THIS
JOURNAL

BELONGS TO:

Simon Price

LITERARY JOURNEYS

A READER'S JOURNAL

Illustrated by André Letria

CHRONICLE BOOKS

SAN FRANCISCO

ISBN 978-1-4521-5559-3

Manufactured in China

Design by Kayla Ferriera
Typeset in Stomper and Sanchez

10 9 8 7 6 5 4

Chronicle Books LLC
680 Second Street
San Francisco, California 94107
www.chroniclebooks.com

Chronicle Books publishes distinctive books and gifts. From
award-winning children's titles, bestselling cookbooks, and eclectic
pop culture to acclaimed works of art and design, stationery, and
journals, we craft publishing that's instantly recognizable
for its spirit and creativity. Enjoy our publishing and become
part of our community at www.chroniclebooks.com.

Special quantity discounts are available to corporations and
other organizations. Contact our premiums department at
corporatesales@chroniclebooks.com or at 1-800-759-0190.

A READER'S JOURNAL

There is magic in books. They carry us on long journeys, light our way, and make our hearts soar. They can whisk us away to far-off places or allow us to see more clearly where we really are. A book is a trusted companion and a guide whose wisdom we never want to forget.

Use this reader's journal as a place to collect all the joys and insights you have found in literature. The "Book Notes" pages allow you to log each book you read, with space for notes about the plot and characters, and room to jot down notable quotations so you never forget what you loved about each book. Keep a running list of what you want to read next in the "Books to Check Out" section. There are blank pages in the "Notes, Ideas, and Observations" section, to capture thoughts that don't pertain to a specific book. And at the back, in the "Reading Inspiration" section, are lists of literary prizewinners—plus room for you to create a list of your own personal prizeworthy reads.

Great books await! Begin your journey now.

BOOK NOTES

Book Title: Diary of Ann Frank

Author: Ann Frank

Plot Notes: _____

_____

_____

_____

_____

_____

Character Notes: _____

_____

_____

_____

_____

Favorite Quotes: _____

_____

_____

_____

_____

Other Books to Read by This Author: uhhhh..... N/A

_____

_____

Book Title: The Hunger Games

Author: Suzan Collins

Plot Notes: _____

_____

_____

_____

_____

_____

Character Notes: _____

_____

_____

_____

_____

Favorite Quotes: _____

_____

_____

_____

_____

Other Books to Read by This Author: _____

_____

_____

DATE STARTED

___ / ___ / ___

DATE FINISHED

___ / ___ / ___

° RATE THIS BOOK °

1 2 3 4 5

Book Title: _____

_____

Author: _____

_____

Plot Notes: _____

_____

_____

_____

_____

_____

Character Notes: _____

_____

_____

_____

_____

_____

Favorite Quotes: _____

_____

_____

_____

_____

_____

Other Books to Read by This Author: _____

_____

_____

Book Title: _____

_____

Author: _____

_____

Plot Notes: _____

_____

_____

_____

_____

_____

Character Notes: _____

_____

_____

_____

_____

Favorite Quotes: _____

_____

_____

_____

_____

Other Books to Read by This Author: _____

_____

_____

DATE STARTED

___ / ___ / ___

DATE FINISHED

___ / ___ / ___

° RATE THIS BOOK °

1 2 3 4 5

Book Title: _____

_____

Author: _____

_____

Plot Notes: _____

_____

_____

_____

_____

_____

_____

Character Notes: _____

_____

_____

_____

_____

_____

Favorite Quotes: _____

_____

_____

_____

_____

_____

Other Books to Read by This Author: _____

_____

_____

Book Title: _____

_____

Author: _____

_____

Plot Notes: _____

_____

_____

_____

_____

_____

_____

Character Notes: _____

_____

_____

_____

_____

_____

Favorite Quotes: _____

_____

_____

_____

_____

_____

Other Books to Read by This Author: _____

_____

_____

DATE STARTED

___ / ___ / ___

DATE FINISHED

___ / ___ / ___

◦ **RATE THIS BOOK** ◦

1 2 3 4 5

Book Title: _____

_____

Author: _____

_____

Plot Notes: _____

_____

_____

_____

_____

_____

_____

Character Notes: _____

_____

_____

_____

_____

_____

Favorite Quotes: _____

_____

_____

_____

_____

_____

Other Books to Read by This Author: _____

_____

_____

DATE STARTED

___ / ___ / ___

Book Title: _____

DATE FINISHED

___ / ___ / ___

_____

Author: _____

° RATE THIS BOOK °

1 2 3 4 5

_____

Plot Notes: _____

_____

_____

_____

_____

_____

Character Notes: _____

_____

_____

_____

_____

Favorite Quotes: _____

_____

_____

_____

_____

Other Books to Read by This Author: _____

_____

_____

DATE STARTED

___ / ___ / ___

DATE FINISHED

___ / ___ / ___

° RATE THIS BOOK °

1 2 3 4 5

Book Title: _____

_____

Author: _____

_____

Plot Notes: _____

_____

_____

_____

_____

_____

Character Notes: _____

_____

_____

_____

_____

Favorite Quotes: _____

_____

_____

_____

_____

Other Books to Read by This Author: _____

_____

_____

Book Title: _____

_____

Author: _____

_____

Plot Notes: _____

_____

_____

_____

_____

_____

Character Notes: _____

_____

_____

_____

_____

Favorite Quotes: _____

_____

_____

_____

_____

Other Books to Read by This Author: _____

_____

_____

DATE STARTED

___ / ___ / ___

DATE FINISHED

___ / ___ / ___

° RATE THIS BOOK °

1 2 3 4 5

Book Title: _____

_____

Author: _____

_____

Plot Notes: _____

_____

_____

_____

_____

_____

_____

Character Notes: _____

_____

_____

_____

_____

_____

Favorite Quotes: _____

_____

_____

_____

_____

_____

Other Books to Read by This Author: _____

_____

_____

Book Title: _____

_____

Author: _____

Plot Notes: _____

_____

_____

_____

_____

_____

_____

Character Notes: _____

_____

_____

_____

_____

_____

Favorite Quotes: _____

_____

_____

_____

_____

_____

Other Books to Read by This Author: _____

_____

_____

DATE STARTED

___ / ___ / ___

DATE FINISHED

___ / ___ / ___

° RATE THIS BOOK °

1 2 3 4 5

Book Title: _____

_____

Author: _____

_____

Plot Notes: _____

_____

_____

_____

_____

_____

_____

Character Notes: _____

_____

_____

_____

_____

_____

Favorite Quotes: _____

_____

_____

_____

_____

_____

Other Books to Read by This Author: _____

_____

_____

Book Title: _____

_____

Author: _____

_____

Plot Notes: _____

_____

_____

_____

_____

_____

_____

Character Notes: _____

_____

_____

_____

_____

_____

Favorite Quotes: _____

_____

_____

_____

_____

_____

Other Books to Read by This Author: _____

_____

_____

DATE STARTED

___ / ___ / ___

DATE FINISHED

___ / ___ / ___

° RATE THIS BOOK °

1 2 3 4 5

Book Title: _____

_____

Author: _____

_____

Plot Notes: _____

_____

_____

_____

_____

_____

Character Notes: _____

_____

_____

_____

_____

Favorite Quotes: _____

_____

_____

_____

_____

Other Books to Read by This Author: _____

_____

_____

Book Title: _____

_____

Author: _____

_____

Plot Notes: _____

_____

_____

_____

_____

_____

Character Notes: _____

_____

_____

_____

_____

Favorite Quotes: _____

_____

_____

_____

_____

Other Books to Read by This Author: _____

_____

_____

DATE STARTED

___ / ___ / ___

DATE FINISHED

___ / ___ / ___

° RATE THIS BOOK °

1 2 3 4 5

Book Title: _____

_____

Author: _____

_____

Plot Notes: _____

_____

_____

_____

_____

_____

_____

Character Notes: _____

_____

_____

_____

_____

_____

Favorite Quotes: _____

_____

_____

_____

_____

_____

Other Books to Read by This Author: _____

_____

_____

Book Title: _____

_____

Author: _____

_____

Plot Notes: _____

_____

_____

_____

_____

_____

_____

Character Notes: _____

_____

_____

_____

_____

_____

Favorite Quotes: _____

_____

_____

_____

_____

Other Books to Read by This Author: _____

_____

_____

DATE STARTED

___ / ___ / ___

DATE FINISHED

___ / ___ / ___

° RATE THIS BOOK °

1 2 3 4 5

Book Title: _____

_____

Author: _____

_____

Plot Notes: _____

_____

_____

_____

_____

_____

Character Notes: _____

_____

_____

_____

_____

Favorite Quotes: _____

_____

_____

_____

_____

Other Books to Read by This Author: _____

_____

_____

Book Title: _____

_____

Author: _____

_____

Plot Notes: _____

_____

_____

_____

_____

_____

_____

Character Notes: _____

_____

_____

_____

_____

Favorite Quotes: _____

_____

_____

_____

_____

Other Books to Read by This Author: _____

_____

_____

DATE STARTED

___ / ___ / ___

DATE FINISHED

___ / ___ / ___

° RATE THIS BOOK °

1 2 3 4 5

Book Title: _____

_____

Author: _____

_____

Plot Notes: _____

_____

_____

_____

_____

_____

Character Notes: _____

_____

_____

_____

_____

Favorite Quotes: _____

_____

_____

_____

_____

Other Books to Read by This Author: _____

_____

_____

∘ RATE THIS BOOK ∘

1 2 3 4 5

Book Title: _____

_____

Author: _____

_____

Plot Notes: _____

_____

_____

_____

_____

_____

_____

Character Notes: _____

_____

_____

_____

_____

_____

Favorite Quotes: _____

_____

_____

_____

_____

_____

Other Books to Read by This Author: _____

_____

_____

DATE STARTED

__ / __ / __

DATE FINISHED

__ / __ / __

° RATE THIS BOOK °

1 2 3 4 5

Book Title: _____

_____

Author: _____

_____

Plot Notes: _____

_____

_____

_____

_____

_____

_____

Character Notes: _____

_____

_____

_____

_____

Favorite Quotes: _____

_____

_____

_____

_____

Other Books to Read by This Author: _____

_____

_____

Book Title: _____

_____

Author: _____

_____

Plot Notes: _____

_____

_____

_____

_____

_____

Character Notes: _____

_____

_____

_____

_____

Favorite Quotes: _____

_____

_____

_____

_____

Other Books to Read by This Author: _____

_____

_____

DATE STARTED

___ / ___ / ___

DATE FINISHED

___ / ___ / ___

° RATE THIS BOOK °

1 2 3 4 5

Book Title: _____

_____

Author: _____

_____

Plot Notes: _____

_____

_____

_____

_____

_____

_____

Character Notes: _____

_____

_____

_____

_____

Favorite Quotes: _____

_____

_____

_____

_____

Other Books to Read by This Author: _____

_____

_____

Book Title: _____

_____

Author: _____

_____

Plot Notes: _____

_____

_____

_____

_____

_____

Character Notes: _____

_____

_____

_____

_____

Favorite Quotes: _____

_____

_____

_____

_____

Other Books to Read by This Author: _____

_____

_____

DATE STARTED

___ / ___ / ___

DATE FINISHED

___ / ___ / ___

° RATE THIS BOOK °

1 2 3 4 5

Book Title: _____

_____

Author: _____

_____

Plot Notes: _____

_____

_____

_____

_____

_____

_____

Character Notes: _____

_____

_____

_____

_____

_____

Favorite Quotes: _____

_____

_____

_____

_____

_____

Other Books to Read by This Author: _____

_____

_____

DATE STARTED

__ / __ / __

DATE FINISHED

__ / __ / __

° RATE THIS BOOK °

1 2 3 4 5

Book Title: _____

_____

Author: _____

_____

Plot Notes: _____

_____

_____

_____

_____

_____

Character Notes: _____

_____

_____

_____

_____

Favorite Quotes: _____

_____

_____

_____

_____

Other Books to Read by This Author: _____

_____

_____

DATE STARTED

___ / ___ / ___

DATE FINISHED

___ / ___ / ___

° RATE THIS BOOK °

1 2 3 4 5

Book Title: _____

_____

Author: _____

_____

Plot Notes: _____

_____

_____

_____

_____

_____

_____

Character Notes: _____

_____

_____

_____

_____

_____

Favorite Quotes: _____

_____

_____

_____

_____

_____

Other Books to Read by This Author: _____

_____

_____

Book Title: _____

_____

Author: _____

_____

Plot Notes: _____

_____

_____

_____

_____

_____

_____

Character Notes: _____

_____

_____

_____

_____

Favorite Quotes: _____

_____

_____

_____

_____

Other Books to Read by This Author: _____

_____

_____

DATE STARTED

___ / ___ / ___

DATE FINISHED

___ / ___ / ___

∘ RATE THIS BOOK ∘

1 2 3 4 5

DATE STARTED

___ / ___ / ___

DATE FINISHED

___ / ___ / ___

° RATE THIS BOOK °

1 2 3 4 5

Book Title: _____

_____

Author: _____

_____

Plot Notes: _____

_____

_____

_____

_____

_____

_____

Character Notes: _____

_____

_____

_____

_____

Favorite Quotes: _____

_____

_____

_____

_____

Other Books to Read by This Author: _____

_____

_____

Book Title: _____

_____

Author: _____

_____

Plot Notes: _____

_____

_____

_____

_____

_____

Character Notes: _____

_____

_____

_____

_____

Favorite Quotes: _____

_____

_____

_____

_____

Other Books to Read by This Author: _____

_____

_____

DATE STARTED

___ / ___ / ___

DATE FINISHED

___ / ___ / ___

° RATE THIS BOOK °

1 2 3 4 5

Book Title: _____

_____

Author: _____

_____

Plot Notes: _____

_____

_____

_____

_____

_____

Character Notes: _____

_____

_____

_____

_____

_____

Favorite Quotes: _____

_____

_____

_____

_____

Other Books to Read by This Author: _____

_____

_____

Book Title: _____

_____

Author: _____

_____

Plot Notes: _____

_____

_____

_____

_____

_____

Character Notes: _____

_____

_____

_____

_____

_____

Favorite Quotes: _____

_____

_____

_____

_____

Other Books to Read by This Author: _____

_____

_____

Book Title: _____

_____

Author: _____

Plot Notes: _____

_____

_____

_____

_____

_____

Character Notes: _____

_____

_____

_____

_____

Favorite Quotes: _____

_____

_____

_____

_____

Other Books to Read by This Author: _____

_____

_____

Book Title: _____

_____

Author: _____

_____

Plot Notes: _____

_____

_____

_____

_____

_____

Character Notes: _____

_____

_____

_____

_____

Favorite Quotes: _____

_____

_____

_____

_____

Other Books to Read by This Author: _____

_____

_____

DATE STARTED

___ / ___ / ___

DATE FINISHED

___ / ___ / ___

° RATE THIS BOOK °

1 2 3 4 5

Book Title: _____

_____

Author: _____

_____

Plot Notes: _____

_____

_____

_____

_____

_____

_____

Character Notes: _____

_____

_____

_____

_____

Favorite Quotes: _____

_____

_____

_____

_____

Other Books to Read by This Author: _____

_____

_____

Book Title: _____

_____

Author: _____

_____

Plot Notes: _____

_____

_____

_____

_____

_____

Character Notes: _____

_____

_____

_____

_____

Favorite Quotes: _____

_____

_____

_____

_____

Other Books to Read by This Author: _____

_____

_____

DATE STARTED

___ / ___ / ___

DATE FINISHED

___ / ___ / ___

° RATE THIS BOOK °

1 2 3 4 5

Book Title: _____

_____

Author: _____

_____

Plot Notes: _____

_____

_____

_____

_____

_____

Character Notes: _____

_____

_____

_____

_____

Favorite Quotes: _____

_____

_____

_____

_____

Other Books to Read by This Author: _____

_____

_____

Book Title: _____

_____

Author: _____

_____

Plot Notes: _____

_____

_____

_____

_____

_____

Character Notes: _____

_____

_____

_____

_____

Favorite Quotes: _____

_____

_____

_____

_____

Other Books to Read by This Author: _____

_____

_____

DATE STARTED

___ / ___ / ___

DATE FINISHED

___ / ___ / ___

◦ RATE THIS BOOK ◦

1 2 3 4 5

Book Title: _____

_____

Author: _____

_____

Plot Notes: _____

_____

_____

_____

_____

_____

Character Notes: _____

_____

_____

_____

_____

Favorite Quotes: _____

_____

_____

_____

_____

Other Books to Read by This Author: _____

_____

_____

Book Title: _____

_____

Author: _____

_____

Plot Notes: _____

_____

_____

_____

_____

_____

Character Notes: _____

_____

_____

_____

_____

_____

Favorite Quotes: _____

_____

_____

_____

_____

Other Books to Read by This Author: _____

_____

_____

DATE STARTED

___ / ___ / ___

DATE FINISHED

___ / ___ / ___

° RATE THIS BOOK °

1 2 3 4 5

Book Title: _____

_____

Author: _____

Plot Notes: _____

_____

_____

_____

_____

_____

Character Notes: _____

_____

_____

_____

_____

Favorite Quotes: _____

_____

_____

_____

_____

Other Books to Read by This Author: _____

_____

_____

Book Title: _____

_____

Author: _____

_____

Plot Notes: _____

_____

_____

_____

_____

_____

Character Notes: _____

_____

_____

_____

_____

Favorite Quotes: _____

_____

_____

_____

_____

Other Books to Read by This Author: _____

_____

_____

DATE STARTED

___ / ___ / ___

DATE FINISHED

___ / ___ / ___

∘ RATE THIS BOOK ∘

1 2 3 4 5

Book Title: _____

_____

Author: _____

_____

Plot Notes: _____

_____

_____

_____

_____

_____

Character Notes: _____

_____

_____

_____

_____

Favorite Quotes: _____

_____

_____

_____

_____

Other Books to Read by This Author: _____

_____

_____

DATE STARTED

__ / __ / __

DATE FINISHED

__ / __ / __

° RATE THIS BOOK °

1 2 3 4 5

Book Title: _____

_____

Author: _____

_____

Plot Notes: _____

_____

_____

_____

_____

_____

_____

Character Notes: _____

_____

_____

_____

_____

_____

Favorite Quotes: _____

_____

_____

_____

_____

Other Books to Read by This Author: _____

_____

_____

DATE STARTED

___ / ___ / ___

DATE FINISHED

___ / ___ / ___

◦ RATE THIS BOOK ◦

1 2 3 4 5

Book Title: _____

_____

Author: _____

_____

Plot Notes: _____

_____

_____

_____

_____

_____

Character Notes: _____

_____

_____

_____

_____

_____

Favorite Quotes: _____

_____

_____

_____

_____

_____

Other Books to Read by This Author: _____

_____

_____

Book Title: _____

_____

Author: _____

_____

Plot Notes: _____

_____

_____

_____

_____

_____

_____

Character Notes: _____

_____

_____

_____

_____

Favorite Quotes: _____

_____

_____

_____

_____

Other Books to Read by This Author: _____

_____

_____

° RATE THIS BOOK °

1 2 3 4 5

Book Title: _____

_____

Author: _____

_____

Plot Notes: _____

_____

_____

_____

_____

_____

Character Notes: _____

_____

_____

_____

_____

Favorite Quotes: _____

_____

_____

_____

_____

Other Books to Read by This Author: _____

_____

_____

Book Title: _____

_____

Author: _____

_____

Plot Notes: _____

_____

_____

_____

_____

_____

_____

Character Notes: _____

_____

_____

_____

_____

_____

Favorite Quotes: _____

_____

_____

_____

_____

_____

Other Books to Read by This Author: _____

_____

_____

DATE STARTED

___ / ___ / ___

DATE FINISHED

___ / ___ / ___

° RATE THIS BOOK °

1 2 3 4 5

Book Title: _____

_____

Author: _____

_____

Plot Notes: _____

_____

_____

_____

_____

_____

Character Notes: _____

_____

_____

_____

_____

Favorite Quotes: _____

_____

_____

_____

_____

Other Books to Read by This Author: _____

_____

_____

Book Title: _____

_____

Author: _____

_____

Plot Notes: _____

_____

_____

_____

_____

_____

Character Notes: _____

_____

_____

_____

_____

Favorite Quotes: _____

_____

_____

_____

_____

Other Books to Read by This Author: _____

_____

_____

Book Title: _____

_____

Author: _____

_____

Plot Notes: _____

_____

_____

_____

_____

_____

_____

Character Notes: _____

_____

_____

_____

_____

Favorite Quotes: _____

_____

_____

_____

_____

Other Books to Read by This Author: _____

_____

_____

DATE STARTED

__ / __ / __

DATE FINISHED

__ / __ / __

∘ RATE THIS BOOK ∘

1 2 3 4 5

Book Title: _____

_____

Author: _____

_____

Plot Notes: _____

_____

_____

_____

_____

_____

Character Notes: _____

_____

_____

_____

_____

Favorite Quotes: _____

_____

_____

_____

_____

Other Books to Read by This Author: _____

_____

_____

Book Title: _____

_____

Author: _____

_____

Plot Notes: _____

_____

_____

_____

_____

_____

Character Notes: _____

_____

_____

_____

_____

Favorite Quotes: _____

_____

_____

_____

_____

Other Books to Read by This Author: _____

_____

_____

Book Title: _____

_____

Author: _____

_____

Plot Notes: _____

_____

_____

_____

_____

_____

Character Notes: _____

_____

_____

_____

_____

Favorite Quotes: _____

_____

_____

_____

_____

Other Books to Read by This Author: _____

_____

_____

DATE STARTED

___ / ___ / ___

DATE FINISHED

___ / ___ / ___

∘ RATE THIS BOOK ∘

1 2 3 4 5

DATE STARTED

___ / ___ / ___

DATE FINISHED

___ / ___ / ___

° RATE THIS BOOK °

1 2 3 4 5

Book Title: _____

_____

Author: _____

_____

Plot Notes: _____

_____

_____

_____

_____

_____

_____

Character Notes: _____

_____

_____

_____

_____

_____

Favorite Quotes: _____

_____

_____

_____

_____

_____

Other Books to Read by This Author: _____

_____

_____

Book Title: _____

_____

Author: _____

_____

Plot Notes: _____

_____

_____

_____

_____

_____

_____

Character Notes: _____

_____

_____

_____

_____

_____

Favorite Quotes: _____

_____

_____

_____

_____

_____

Other Books to Read by This Author: _____

_____

_____

DATE STARTED

___ / ___ / ___

DATE FINISHED

___ / ___ / ___

° RATE THIS BOOK °

1 2 3 4 5

Book Title: _____

_____

Author: _____

_____

Plot Notes: _____

_____

_____

_____

_____

_____

Character Notes: _____

_____

_____

_____

_____

Favorite Quotes: _____

_____

_____

_____

_____

Other Books to Read by This Author: _____

_____

_____

Book Title: _____

_____

Author: _____

_____

Plot Notes: _____

_____

_____

_____

_____

_____

Character Notes: _____

_____

_____

_____

_____

Favorite Quotes: _____

_____

_____

_____

_____

Other Books to Read by This Author: _____

_____

_____

DATE STARTED

__ / __ / __

DATE FINISHED

__ / __ / __

° RATE THIS BOOK °

1 2 3 4 5

DATE STARTED

___ / ___ / ___

DATE FINISHED

___ / ___ / ___

∘ RATE THIS BOOK ∘

1 2 3 4 5

Book Title: _____

_____

Author: _____

_____

Plot Notes: _____

_____

_____

_____

_____

_____

Character Notes: _____

_____

_____

_____

_____

Favorite Quotes: _____

_____

_____

_____

_____

Other Books to Read by This Author: _____

_____

_____

DATE STARTED

___ / ___ / ___

DATE FINISHED

___ / ___ / ___

° RATE THIS BOOK °

1 2 3 4 5

Book Title: _____

_____

Author: _____

_____

Plot Notes: _____

_____

_____

_____

_____

_____

_____

Character Notes: _____

_____

_____

_____

_____

_____

Favorite Quotes: _____

_____

_____

_____

_____

Other Books to Read by This Author: _____

_____

_____

DATE STARTED

___ / ___ / ___

DATE FINISHED

___ / ___ / ___

° RATE THIS BOOK °

1 2 3 4 5

Book Title: _____

_____

Author: _____

_____

Plot Notes: _____

_____

_____

_____

_____

_____

Character Notes: _____

_____

_____

_____

_____

Favorite Quotes: _____

_____

_____

_____

_____

Other Books to Read by This Author: _____

_____

_____

Book Title: _____

_____

Author: _____

_____

Plot Notes: _____

_____

_____

_____

_____

_____

Character Notes: _____

_____

_____

_____

_____

Favorite Quotes: _____

_____

_____

_____

_____

Other Books to Read by This Author: _____

_____

_____

DATE STARTED

__ / __ / __

DATE FINISHED

__ / __ / __

∘ RATE THIS BOOK ∘

1 2 3 4 5

Book Title: _____

_____

Author: _____

_____

Plot Notes: _____

_____

_____

_____

_____

_____

Character Notes: _____

_____

_____

_____

_____

Favorite Quotes: _____

_____

_____

_____

_____

Other Books to Read by This Author: _____

_____

_____

Book Title: _____

_____

Author: _____

_____

Plot Notes: _____

_____

_____

_____

_____

_____

Character Notes: _____

_____

_____

_____

_____

Favorite Quotes: _____

_____

_____

_____

_____

Other Books to Read by This Author: _____

_____

_____

DATE STARTED

___ / ___ / ___

DATE FINISHED

___ / ___ / ___

∘ RATE THIS BOOK ∘

1 2 3 4 5

Book Title: _____

_____

Author: _____

_____

Plot Notes: _____

_____

_____

_____

_____

_____

Character Notes: _____

_____

_____

_____

_____

Favorite Quotes: _____

_____

_____

_____

_____

Other Books to Read by This Author: _____

_____

_____

Book Title: _____

_____

Author: _____

_____

Plot Notes: _____

_____

_____

_____

_____

_____

Character Notes: _____

_____

_____

_____

_____

_____

Favorite Quotes: _____

_____

_____

_____

_____

_____

Other Books to Read by This Author: _____

_____

_____

Book Title: _____

_____

Author: _____

_____

Plot Notes: _____

_____

_____

_____

_____

_____

Character Notes: _____

_____

_____

_____

_____

Favorite Quotes: _____

_____

_____

_____

_____

Other Books to Read by This Author: _____

_____

_____

DATE STARTED

___ / ___ / ___

DATE FINISHED

___ / ___ / ___

∘ RATE THIS BOOK ∘

1 2 3 4 5

Book Title: _____

_____

Author: _____

_____

Plot Notes: _____

_____

_____

_____

_____

_____

Character Notes: _____

_____

_____

_____

_____

Favorite Quotes: _____

_____

_____

_____

_____

Other Books to Read by This Author: _____

_____

_____

DATE STARTED

___ / ___ / ___

DATE FINISHED

___ / ___ / ___

° RATE THIS BOOK °

1 2 3 4 5

Book Title: _____

_____

Author: _____

_____

Plot Notes: _____

_____

_____

_____

_____

_____

Character Notes: _____

_____

_____

_____

_____

Favorite Quotes: _____

_____

_____

_____

_____

Other Books to Read by This Author: _____

_____

_____

Book Title: _____

_____

Author: _____

_____

Plot Notes: _____

_____

_____

_____

_____

_____

Character Notes: _____

_____

_____

_____

_____

Favorite Quotes: _____

_____

_____

_____

_____

Other Books to Read by This Author: _____

_____

_____

DATE STARTED

___ / ___ / ___

DATE FINISHED

___ / ___ / ___

° RATE THIS BOOK °

1 2 3 4 5

Book Title: _____

_____

Author: _____

_____

Plot Notes: _____

_____

_____

_____

_____

_____

Character Notes: _____

_____

_____

_____

_____

Favorite Quotes: _____

_____

_____

_____

_____

Other Books to Read by This Author: _____

_____

_____

Book Title: _____

_____

Author: _____

_____

Plot Notes: _____

_____

_____

_____

_____

_____

Character Notes: _____

_____

_____

_____

_____

Favorite Quotes: _____

_____

_____

_____

_____

Other Books to Read by This Author: _____

_____

_____

BOOKS TO CHECK OUT

Book Title: _____

Author: _____

Notes: _____

_____

_____

Book Title: _____

Author: _____

Notes: _____

_____

_____

Book Title: _____

Author: _____

Notes: _____

_____

_____

Book Title: _____

Author: _____

Notes: _____

_____

_____

Book Title: _____

Author: _____

Notes: _____

_____

_____

Book Title: _____

Author: _____

Notes: _____

_____

_____

Book Title: _____

Author: _____

Notes: _____

_____

_____

Book Title: _____

Author: _____

Notes: _____

_____

_____

Book Title: _____

Author: _____

Notes: _____

_____

_____

Book Title: _____

Author: _____

Notes: _____

_____

_____

Book Title: _____

Author: _____

Notes: _____

_____

_____

Book Title: _____

Author: _____

Notes: _____

_____

_____

Book Title: _____

Author: _____

Notes: _____

_____

_____

Book Title: _____

Author: _____

Notes: _____

_____

_____

Book Title: _____

Author: _____

Notes: _____

_____

_____

Book Title: _____

Author: _____

Notes: _____

_____

_____

Book Title: _____

Author: _____

Notes: _____

_____

_____

Book Title: _____

Author: _____

Notes: _____

_____

_____

Book Title: _____

Author: _____

Notes: _____

_____

_____

Book Title: _____

Author: _____

Notes: _____

_____

_____

Book Title: _____

Author: _____

Notes: _____

_____

_____

Book Title: _____

Author: _____

Notes: _____

_____

_____

Book Title: _____

Author: _____

Notes: _____

_____

_____

Book Title: _____

Author: _____

Notes: _____

_____

_____

Book Title: _____

Author: _____

Notes: _____

_____

_____

Book Title: _____

Author: _____

Notes: _____

_____

_____

Book Title: _____

Author: _____

Notes: _____

_____

_____

Book Title: _____

Author: _____

Notes: _____

_____

_____

Book Title: _____

Author: _____

Notes: _____

_____

_____

Book Title: _____

Author: _____

Notes: _____

_____

_____

Book Title: _____

Author: _____

Notes: _____

_____

_____

Book Title: _____

Author: _____

Notes: _____

_____

_____

Book Title: _____

Author: _____

Notes: _____

_____

_____

Book Title: _____

Author: _____

Notes: _____

_____

_____

Book Title: _____

Author: _____

Notes: _____

_____

_____

Book Title: _____

Author: _____

Notes: _____

_____

_____

BOOKS TO CHECK OUT

Book Title: _____

Author: _____

Notes: _____

_____

_____

Book Title: _____

Author: _____

Notes: _____

_____

_____

Book Title: _____

Author: _____

Notes: _____

_____

_____

Book Title: _____

Author: _____

Notes: _____

_____

_____

Book Title: _____

Author: _____

Notes: _____

_____

_____

Book Title: _____

Author: _____

Notes: _____

_____

_____

Book Title: _____

Author: _____

Notes: _____

_____

_____

Book Title: _____

Author: _____

Notes: _____

_____

_____

Book Title: _____

Author: _____

Notes: _____

_____

_____

Book Title: _____

Author: _____

Notes: _____

_____

_____

Book Title: _____

Author: _____

Notes: _____

_____

_____

Book Title: _____

Author: _____

Notes: _____

_____

_____

Book Title: _____

Author: _____

Notes: _____

_____

_____

Book Title: _____

Author: _____

Notes: _____

_____

_____

Book Title: _____

Author: _____

Notes: _____

_____

_____

Book Title: _____

Author: _____

Notes: _____

_____

_____

Book Title: _____

Author: _____

Notes: _____

_____

_____

Book Title: _____

Author: _____

Notes: _____

_____

_____

Book Title: _____

Author: _____

Notes: _____

_____

_____

Book Title: _____

Author: _____

Notes: _____

_____

_____

NOTES, IDEAS, AND OBSERVATIONS

NOTES · IDEAS · OBSERVATIONS

NOTES · IDEAS · OBSERVATIONS

NOTES · IDEAS · OBSERVATIONS

NOTES · IDEAS · OBSERVATIONS

NOTES · IDEAS · OBSERVATIONS

NOTES · IDEAS · OBSERVATIONS

NOTES · IDEAS · OBSERVATIONS

NOTES · IDEAS · OBSERVATIONS

NOTES · IDEAS · OBSERVATIONS

NOTES · IDEAS · OBSERVATIONS

READING INSPIRATION

READING INSPIRATION

The last page, the last line—how bittersweet it is to finish a book! Choosing your next read is the only salve. If you don't have a new book on deck, here's a sampling of prizewinners from some of the major literary awards. These lists are by no means exhaustive, but perhaps your next favorite book will be among them.

NATIONAL BOOK AWARD FOR FICTION

The National Book Foundation rewards American writers (of many different genres, although here we cite only fiction) of exceptional merit. (www.nationalbook.org)

1950 *The Man with the Golden Arm*, Nelson Algren

1951 *The Collected Stories of William Faulkner*, William Faulkner

1952 *From Here to Eternity*, James Jones

1953 *Invisible Man*, Ralph Ellison

1954 *The Adventures of Augie March*, Saul Bellow

1955 *A Fable*, William Faulkner

1956 *Ten North Frederick*, John O'Hara

1957 *The Field of Vision*, Wright Morris

1958 *The Wapshot Chronicle*, John Cheever

1959 *The Magic Barrel*, Bernard Malamud

1960 *Goodbye, Columbus*, Philip Roth

1961 *The Waters of Kronos*, Conrad Richter

1962 *The Moviegoer*, Walker Percy

1963 *Morte D'Urban*, J. F. Powers

1964 *The Centaur*, John Updike

1965 *Herzog*, Saul Bellow

1966 *The Collected Stories of Katherine Anne Porter*, Katherine Anne Porter

MAN BOOKER PRIZE

The Man Booker Prize is awarded to a novel written in English and published in the United Kingdom. (www.themanbookerprize.com)

PEN/FAULKNER AWARD FOR FICTION

The PEN/Faulkner Award for Fiction is awarded to living American fiction writers. (www.penfaulkner.org)

1991 *Philadelphia Fire*, John Edgar Wideman
1992 *Mao II*, Don DeLillo
1993 *Postcards*, E. Annie Proulx
1994 *Operation Shylock*, Philip Roth
1995 *Snow Falling on Cedars*, David Guterson
1996 *Independence Day*, Richard Ford
1997 *Women in Their Beds*, Gina Berriault
1998 *The Bear Comes Home*, Rafi Zabor
1999 *The Hours*, Michael Cunningham
2000 *Waiting*, Ha Jin
2001 *The Human Stain*, Philip Roth
2002 *Bel Canto*, Ann Patchett
2003 *The Caprices*, Sabina Murray
2004 *The Early Stories: 1953–1975*, John Updike
2005 *War Trash*, Ha Jin
2006 *The March*, E. L. Doctorow
2007 *Everyman*, Philip Roth
2008 *The Great Man*, Kate Christensen
2009 *Netherland*, Joseph O'Neill
2010 *War Dances*, Sherman Alexie
2011 *The Collected Stories of Deborah Eisenberg*,
       Deborah Eisenberg
2012 *The Buddha in the Attic*, Julie Otsuka
2013 *Everything Begins & Ends at the Kentucky Club*,
       Benjamin Alire Sáenz
2014 *We Are All Completely Beside Ourselves*, Karen Joy Fowler
2015 *Preparation for the Next Life*, Atticus Lish

PULITZER PRIZE FOR FICTION

The Pulitzer Prizes are awarded in many different categories, most famously for journalism. The Pulitzer for fiction is awarded for "distinguished fiction by an American author, preferably dealing with American life." No Pulitzer prizes for fiction were awarded for the years 1954, 1957, 1964, 1971, 1974, 1977, and 2012. (www.pulitzer.org)

1948 *Tales of the South Pacific*, James A. Michener

1949 *Guard of Honor*, James Gould Cozzens

1950 *The Way West*, A. B. Guthrie, Jr.

1951 *The Town*, Conrad Richter

1952 *The Caine Mutiny*, Herman Wouk

1953 *The Old Man and the Sea*, Ernest Hemingway

1955 *A Fable*, William Faulkner

1956 *Andersonville*, MacKinlay Kantor

1958 *A Death in the Family*, James Agee

1959 *The Travels of Jaimie McPheeters*, Robert Lewis Taylor

1960 *Advise and Consent*, Allen Drury

1961 *To Kill a Mockingbird*, Harper Lee

1962 *The Edge of Sadness*, Edwin O'Connor

1963 *The Reivers*, William Faulkner

1965 *The Keepers of the House*, Shirley Ann Grau

1966 *The Collected Stories of Katherine Anne Porter*, Katherine Anne Porter

1967 *The Fixer*, Bernard Malamud

1968 *The Confessions of Nat Turner*, William Styron

1969 *House Made of Dawn*, N. Scott Momaday

1970 *The Collected Stories of Jean Stafford*, Jean Stafford

1972 *Angle of Repose*, Wallace Stegner

1973 *The Optimist's Daughter*, Eudora Welty

1975 *The Killer Angels*, Michael Shaara

1976 *Humboldt's Gift*, Saul Bellow

1978 *Elbow Room*, James Alan McPherson

1979 *The Stories of John Cheever*, John Cheever

1980 *The Executioner's Song*, Norman Mailer

1981 *A Confederacy of Dunces*, John Kennedy Toole

1982 *Rabbit Is Rich*, John Updike

1983 *The Color Purple*, Alice Walker

1984 *Ironweed*, William Kennedy

1985 *Foreign Affairs*, Alison Lurie

1986 *Lonesome Dove*, Larry McMurtry

1987 *A Summons to Memphis*, Peter Taylor

1988 *Beloved*, Toni Morrison

1989 *Breathing Lessons*, Anne Tyler

1990 *The Mambo Kings Play Songs of Love*, Oscar Hijuelos

1991 *Rabbit at Rest*, John Updike

1992 *A Thousand Acres*, Jane Smiley

1993 *A Good Scent from a Strange Mountain*, Robert Olen Butler

1994 *The Shipping News*, E. Annie Proulx

1995 *The Stone Diaries*, Carol Shields

1996 *Independence Day*, Richard Ford

1997 *Martin Dressler: The Tale of an American Dreamer*, by Steven Millhauser

1998 *American Pastoral*, Philip Roth

1999 *The Hours*, Michael Cunningham

2000 *Interpreter of Maladies*, Jhumpa Lahiri

2001 *The Amazing Adventures of Kavalier & Clay*, Michael Chabon

2002 *Empire Falls*, Richard Russo

2003 *Middlesex*, Jeffrey Eugenides

2004 *The Known World*, Edward P. Jones

2005 *Gilead*, Marilynne Robinson

MY PRIZEWINNERS

What books would you award highest honors?

Book Title: _____

Author: _____

Date Read: _____

Book Title: _____

Author: _____

Date Read: _____

Book Title: _____

Author: _____

Date Read: _____

Book Title: _____

Author: _____

Date Read: _____

Book Title: _____

Author: _____

Date Read: _____

Book Title: _____

Author: _____

Date Read: _____

Book Title: _____

Author: _____

Date Read: _____

Book Title: _____

Author: _____

Date Read: _____

Book Title: _____

Author: _____

Date Read: _____

Book Title: _____

Author: _____

Date Read: _____

Book Title: _____

Author: _____

Date Read: _____

Book Title: _____

Author: _____

Date Read: _____

Book Title: _____

Author: _____

Date Read: _____

Book Title: _____

Author: _____

Date Read: _____

Book Title: _____

Author: _____

Date Read: _____

Book Title: _____

Author: _____

Date Read: _____

Book Title: _____

Author: _____

Date Read: _____